ANIMAL EXTREMES

MIND-BOGGLING MAMMALS

BY LIBBY WILSON

WWW.APEXEDITIONS.COM

Copyright © 2024 by Apex Editions, Mendota Heights, MN 55120. All rights reserved. No part of this book may be reproduced or utilized in any form or by any means without written permission from the publisher.

Apex is distributed by North Star Editions:
sales@northstareditions.com | 888-417-0195

Produced for Apex by Red Line Editorial.

Photographs ©: Shutterstock Images, cover, 1, 4–5, 6, 8–9, 10–11, 14–15, 16–17, 18, 19, 20, 21, 22–23, 24, 25, 26, 27, 29; iStockphoto, 13

Library of Congress Control Number: 2022919897

ISBN
978-1-63738-531-9 (hardcover)
978-1-63738-585-2 (paperback)
978-1-63738-692-7 (ebook pdf)
978-1-63738-639-2 (hosted ebook)

Printed in the United States of America
Mankato, MN
082023

NOTE TO PARENTS AND EDUCATORS

Apex books are designed to build literacy skills in striving readers. Exciting, high-interest content attracts and holds readers' attention. The text is carefully leveled to allow students to achieve success quickly. Additional features, such as bolded glossary words for difficult terms, help build comprehension.

TABLE OF CONTENTS

CHAPTER 1
SPRINGY SPRINGBOKS 4

CHAPTER 2
FLYING FURBALLS 10

CHAPTER 3
UNUSUAL EATERS 16

CHAPTER 4
ODD BODIES 22

COMPREHENSION QUESTIONS • 28
GLOSSARY • 30
TO LEARN MORE • 31
ABOUT THE AUTHOR • 31
INDEX • 32

CHAPTER 1

SPRINGY SPRINGBOKS

Several springboks are standing in a field. One animal takes a running hop. It bounds almost 7 feet (2.1 m) into the air.

Springboks are fast runners. They can go 55 miles per hour (88 km/h).

The springbok lands on all four feet at once. Then it bounces into the air again. It does this over and over.

PRONKING

A springbok's high jumping is called pronking. That means "showing off" in Afrikaans. No one is sure why springboks pronk. Sometimes, they may be scared by enemies. Other times, they may be having fun.

◀ Springboks live in dry, grassy areas in southern Africa.

A second springbok joins in. So does another. Soon, the air is filled with leaping animals.

FAST FACT
Springboks can go their whole lives without drinking. They get water from eating plants.

Springboks live in herds. Each group is made up of females, their babies, and a few males.

CHAPTER 2

FLYING FURBALLS

Sifakas are **lemurs**. They use their long back legs to leap from tree to tree. They can jump more than 30 feet (9 m).

Sifakas live in forests on the island of Madagascar

Greater gliders can jump 328 feet (100 m) between trees. Their long tails help them steer as they move through the air.

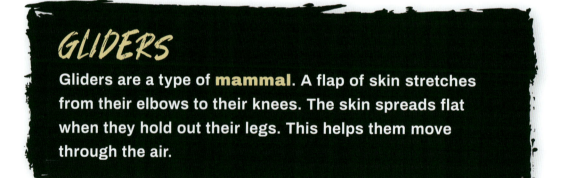

GLIDERS

Gliders are a type of **mammal**. A flap of skin stretches from their elbows to their knees. The skin spreads flat when they hold out their legs. This helps them move through the air.

Greater gliders live in Australia. They're about the same size as pet cats.

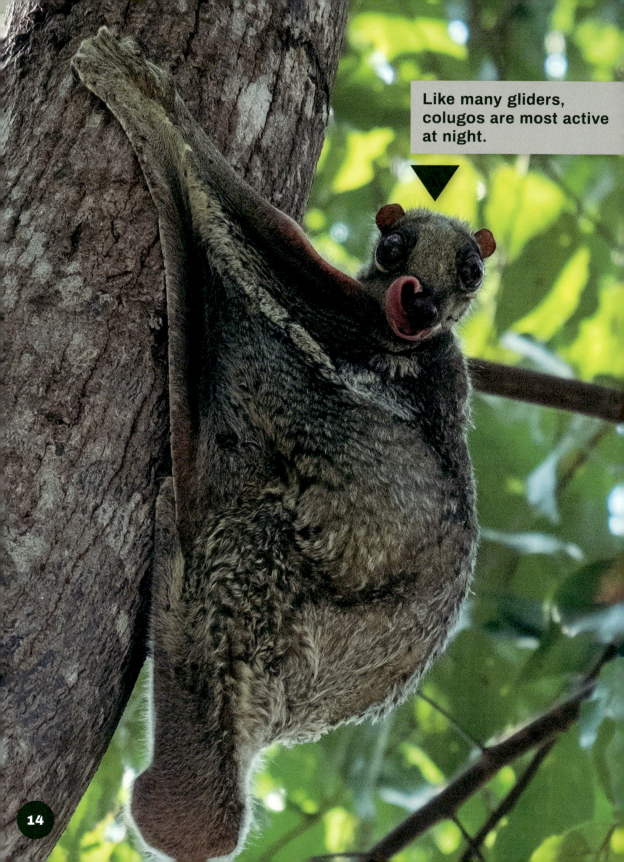

Like many gliders, colugos are most active at night.

14

Scaly-tail gliders can glide for 820 feet (250 m). These small **rodents** live in Africa. Large groups rest together in hollow trees.

FAST FACT

Colugos are **nocturnal** gliders. Huge red eyes help them see in the dark.

CHAPTER 3

Unusual Eaters

Gerenuks stand up on their back legs to eat. Their front legs pull down branches. They can reach leaves 8 feet (2.4 m) high.

Gerenuks live in eastern Africa. They often eat leaves from thorny trees.

Aye-ayes have very long middle fingers. They use these fingers to tap branches. The sounds help them find insect tunnels. Aye-ayes then scoop out insect **larvae** and eat them.

An aye-aye's sharp teeth can bite through tree bark.

FAST FACT

Pygmy shrews have tiny bodies. They eat three times their own weight each day.

Pygmy shrews hunt almost constantly. They sleep for just a few minutes at a time.

Short-beaked echidnas use their claws to dig for insects.

Echidnas eat worms and insects. They use their tongues to grab food. They suck it up through thin snouts.

SEVERAL SPECIES

There are four **species** of echidnas. Some have tongues that are sticky. Others have tongues that are covered in spikes. They help the echidnas grab and smash food.

Long-beaked echidnas don't have teeth. Their tongues crush food instead.

CHAPTER 4

ODD BODIES

Streaked tenrecs have sharp spines on their necks and backs. They use these spines for defense. They poke **predators**.

A streaked tenrec can rub its spines together to make high-pitched sounds.

Chinese water deer don't grow antlers. Instead, males have fangs. These teeth can grow 2 inches (5 cm) long. The deer use them to fight.

Chinese water deer stand about 2 feet (61 cm) tall. They live near rivers.

A full-grown mouse deer is just 12 inches (30 cm) tall.

MOUSE DEER

Mouse deer are the smallest hoofed mammals. They have fangs. But they usually hide from predators. They walk along river bottoms. They can stay underwater for four minutes.

FAST FACT

Platypuses are some of the only mammals that lay eggs. Echidnas are the others.

Platypuses are great swimmers. They often live in lakes and rivers.

A few mammals have **venom**. One is the platypus. It stabs enemies with sharp spurs on its legs. Solenodons and slow lorises bite. Their teeth have venom.

A slow loris's venom comes from a spot on its elbow. The loris licks this spot to get venom on its teeth.

COMPREHENSION QUESTIONS

Write your answers on a separate piece of paper.

1. Write a sentence describing what it means for a springbok to pronk.

2. Which mammal described in the book do you find most interesting? Why?

3. Which mammal lays eggs?
    - **A.** echidna
    - **B.** sifaka
    - **C.** tenrec

4. How could a platypus defend itself from predators?
    - **A.** bite them with its long fangs
    - **B.** poke them with its sharp spines
    - **C.** stab them with its venomous spur

5. What does **bounds** mean in this book?

*One animal takes a running hop. It **bounds** almost 7 feet (2.1 m) into the air.*

    A. jumps up high
    B. crawls down low
    C. stays very still

6. What does **defense** mean in this book?

*They use these spines for **defense**. They poke predators.*

    A. a way to find food
    B. a way to fight back
    C. a way to make sounds

Answer key on page 32.

GLOSSARY

larvae
Insects that have hatched from eggs but have not yet changed to adults.

lemurs
Types of animals that live in trees and have long, furry tails.

mammal
An animal that has hair and produces milk for its young.

nocturnal
Awake and active at night.

predators
Animals that hunt and eat other animals.

rodents
Small, furry animals with large front teeth, such as rats or mice.

species
Groups of animals or plants that are similar and can breed with one another.

venom
A poison made by an animal and used to bite or sting prey.

BOOKS

Bassier, Emma. *Aye-Ayes*. Minneapolis: Abdo Publishing, 2020.

Kenney, Karen Latchana. *Platypuses*. Minneapolis: Bellwether Media, 2021.

Peterson, Megan Cooley. *Freakishly Creepy Creatures*. North Mankato, MN: Capstone Publishing, 2023.

ONLINE RESOURCES

Visit **www.apexeditions.com** to find links and resources related to this title.

ABOUT THE AUTHOR

Libby Wilson is a retired school librarian who has loved books all her life. Her favorite topics to write about are animals, history, and inspirational people.

INDEX

A
aye-ayes, 18

C
Chinese water deer, 24

E
echidnas, 20–21, 26
eggs, 26

F
fangs, 24–25

G
gerenuks, 16
gliders, 12, 15

M
mouse deer, 25

P
platypuses, 26–27
pygmy shrews, 19

S
sifakas, 10
slow lorises, 27
solenodons, 27
springboks, 4, 7, 8–9
streaked tenrecs, 22

V
venom, 27

ANSWER KEY:
1. Answers will vary; 2. Answers will vary; 3. A; 4. C; 5. A; 6. B